DIGITAL MARKETING ACCELERATED:

A Marketer's Guide To Success

Dack Douglas

Icon Publications Limited

CONTENTS

FOREWORD

In the vast ocean of modern marketing, where technology surges like powerful waves, there lies a treasure trove of untapped potential awaiting those who dare to venture into its depths. "Digital Marketing Accelerated: A Marketer's Guide To Success," is an extraordinary voyage, guiding aspiring marketers and seasoned professionals alike on an exhilarating journey to unlock the secrets of digital success.

In this captivating book, the reader is bestowed with the compass of knowledge, generously provided by a masterful guide, to navigate the ever-changing landscape of digital marketing. Like skilled navigators, the authors steer us through the intricate channels of emerging technologies, data-driven insights, and customer-centric strategies that shape the modern marketing realm.

"Digital Marketing Accelerated" is not just another blueprint; it is a symphony of innovative ideas, woven together with the finesse of creativity and the precision of data analytics. As we embark on this expedition, we encounter the allure of AI, the resonance of voice search, and the camaraderie of chatbots, all harmoniously orchestrated to elevate brand experiences and deepen audience connections.

The pages of this book resonate with authenticity, reflecting the authors' passion and expertise in their craft. Their wisdom, acquired through years of hands-on experience and continuous learning, is shared generously with the reader. "Digital Marketing Accelerated" empowers marketers to harness the power of technology while keeping a human touch, creating a harmonious balance between innovation and empathy.

Whether you are a seasoned marketing captain or a budding sailor setting sail in the digital ocean, "Digital Marketing Accelerated " offers invaluable wisdom and insights to steer your vessel towards success. The book's actionable strategies, real-world case studies, and forward-thinking perspectives illuminate the path, guiding you through uncharted waters to seize the untapped potential of modern marketing.

As you dive into these pages, be prepared to embark on a transformational voyage. Equip yourself with the knowledge to navigate the challenges and embrace the opportunities that the digital era presents. "Digital Mastery" is your compass, your guiding star, and your trusty companion as you sail towards excellence in modern marketing.

Bon voyage, dear reader. Prepare to unleash the power of modern marketing, for the journey ahead promises endless possibilities and unparalleled growth.

"DIGITAL MARKETING: ACCELERATED A MARKETER'S GUIDE TO SUCCESS"

Introduction:

In today's rapidly evolving digital landscape, mastering the art of digital marketing is essential for businesses to thrive. This book, "Digital Marketing Accelerated: A Marketer's Guide To Success, " serves as your comprehensive guide to navigate the intricacies of the digital realm, unlocking the potential to reach and engage your target audience like never before. Packed with practical strategies, real-world examples, and expert insights, this book will empower you to become a digital marketing maestro.

CHAPTER 1: FOUNDATIONS OF DIGITAL MARKETING

Understanding The Digital Marketing Ecosystem

To unravel the intricate tapestry of the digital marketing ecosystem, envision it as a dynamic symphony of interconnected instruments. Each instrument represents a crucial element, such as SEO, social media, content creation, and data analytics, harmoniously working together to produce a melodious marketing strategy.

By immersing yourself in this symphony, you'll need to listen attentively to each note, grasping the essence of every instrument's role. Embrace the ever-changing tempo and rhythm, as digital marketing constantly evolves, demanding flexibility and adaptation.

Like a skilled conductor, learn to synchronize the diverse elements, directing them towards a unified goal: engaging the audience and generating meaningful connections. Embrace experimentation, exploring new combinations of instruments, and fine-tune your marketing tactics.

Remember, the art of understanding the digital marketing ecosystem lies not merely in memorizing its components but in grasping the synergy they create as a whole. Embrace the harmony, and you shall orchestrate success in the ever-expanding digital landscape.

Defining Your Target Audience And Setting Goals

In the vast sea of digital marketing, defining your target audience and setting goals is akin to charting a course for a grand voyage. Picture yourself as an intrepid captain, steering your marketing ship with purpose and precision.

Begin by hoisting the sails of research and observation. Delve deep into the waters of data analytics and market research to understand the tides of consumer behavior. Unearth insights that reveal the hidden treasures of your audience's preferences, interests, and pain points.

Next, navigate through the vast expanse of demographics and psychographics, discovering the uncharted territories of your ideal customers. Paint a vivid portrait of your target audience, capturing their personas like portraits hung in the halls of your marketing vessel.

As you set sail, navigate by the stars of specificity. Avoid the treacherous waters of vague generalizations, and instead, steer towards the clarity of a well-defined target audience. Narrow your focus to reach those most likely to resonate with your brand's message.

With your compass calibrated, set ambitious goals as your North Star. Let them shine brightly, guiding your efforts and keeping your crew aligned. Be bold, yet realistic, in your aspirations, for they shall fuel your marketing expedition with purpose and direction.

As you journey forth, remember that the digital marketing seas are ever-changing. Stay agile, and adjust your course as needed to adapt to shifting currents and winds of opportunity. Armed with an intimate knowledge of your target audience and unwavering goals, you shall navigate the digital waters with confidence, charting a path to success.

Crafting A Compelling Brand Identity Online

Crafting a compelling brand identity online for your digital marketing is akin to weaving an intricate tapestry of emotions and impressions that captivate your audience. Imagine yourself as a skilled artisan, meticulously selecting each thread to create a masterpiece that resonates deeply with your customers.

Start by choosing a vibrant and authentic color palette, evoking emotions that mirror your brand's personality. Just as colors infuse life into a canvas, they breathe life into your online presence, leaving a lasting impression on your audience.

Next, carefully sculpt your brand's voice and tone, as though chiseling words from stone. Consistency is key – let your messaging echo throughout every platform, forging a cohesive narrative that strengthens your brand's identity.

Forge a distinctive logo, symbolizing the essence of your brand like a precious gem, recognizable at a glance amidst the digital crowd. Your logo shall become the beacon that guides your audience back to you.
As you embark on this creative journey, remember to imbue your brand with a human touch. Cultivate authentic connections by engaging in meaningful conversations, for your audience seeks genuine interactions that inspire loyalty and trust.

Lastly, like an evergreen tree standing tall against the changing seasons, cultivate consistency in your brand's appearance and messaging. This steadfastness will etch your brand into the memories of your audience, ensuring your presence remains timeless in the digital landscape.

As an artisan of your brand identity, be patient in your craftsmanship and adaptable to refining your masterpiece. With passion and dedication, your online brand identity will stand as a captivating work of art, drawing admiration from a devoted and engaged audience.

* * *

CHAPTER 2: BUILDING A WINNING WEBSITE AND USER EXPERIENCE

Optimizing Your Website For Search Engines

To optimize your website for search engines and elevate your digital marketing business, follow these strategic steps:

1. Keyword Research: Identify relevant and high-traffic keywords related to your business. Use tools like Google Keyword Planner or other SEO platforms to uncover valuable keyword opportunities.

2. On-Page Optimization: Ensure each page of your website has a unique title tag, meta description, and relevant content that incorporates your target keywords naturally. Optimize headings (H1, H2, etc.) and use descriptive URLs.

3. Quality Content: Craft compelling, informative, and valuable content that resonates with your target audience. Aim for longer-form content where appropriate, as search engines often favor in-depth articles.

4. Mobile-Friendly Design: Ensure your website is responsive and adapts seamlessly to various devices, particularly mobile phones, as mobile-friendliness is now a crucial ranking factor.

5. Site Speed: Optimize your website's loading speed by compressing images, leveraging browser caching, and using content delivery networks (CDNs) to enhance user experience and search engine rankings.

6. Link Building: Develop a strong backlink profile by earning links from authoritative and relevant websites. Guest posting, creating shareable content, and networking within your industry can help acquire quality backlinks.

7. User Experience (UX): Create a user-friendly website with intuitive navigation, easy-to-use menus, and clear calls-to-action. Positive user experiences lead to better engagement and search engine ranking.

8. Local SEO: If your digital marketing business serves a specific area, optimize your website for local searches. Set up a Google My Business profile and include your business's name, address, phone number, and operating hours.

9. Meta Tags and Schema Markup: Implement schema markup to provide search engines with additional context about your content. Rich snippets can enhance your search results, increasing click-through rates.

10. Regular Updates: Keep your website fresh and relevant by updating content regularly. Engage with your audience through blogs, news articles, or industry insights, demonstrating your expertise and commitment.

11. Monitor Analytics: Use tools like Google Analytics to track website performance, user behavior, and conversions. Analyzing data will help you identify strengths and weaknesses, allowing you to make informed decisions for improvement.

Remember, SEO is an ongoing process, and it may take time to see significant results. Be patient, stay informed about SEO best practices, and adapt your strategy as needed to stay competitive in the digital marketing landscape.

Designing A User-Friendly Interface And Seamless Navigation

Designing a user-friendly interface and seamless navigation for your website is akin to crafting a virtual oasis where visitors can wander effortlessly through a captivating landscape of information and offerings. Picture yourself as an empathetic architect, sculpting an intuitive structure that beckons users to explore and engage.

Start by understanding the desires and needs of your audience, as a skilled architect studies the habits and aspirations of the inhabitants. Empathy will be your cornerstone, paving the way for a design that anticipates their journey and delivers a smooth and delightful experience.

Create an inviting entrance with a visually appealing and clutter-free homepage, akin to an elegant foyer that welcomes guests warmly. Introduce them to your brand's essence with clear and concise messaging, guiding them to explore further with curiosity.

As users venture deeper into your virtual sanctuary, craft an organized layout like a well-designed city grid, where every street leads to relevant destinations. Ensure logical categorization and intuitive menus, empowering users to find what they seek without wandering aimlessly.

Establish visual harmony with a consistent and aesthetically pleasing color palette, as an architect uses a harmonious blend of materials to construct a pleasing ambiance. Select fonts and graphics that resonate with your brand's personality, reinforcing your digital marketing message.

Illuminate the path with prominent and strategically placed calls-to-action, as thoughtful lampposts guide travelers along their way. Your CTAs should inspire action, leading users to connect, subscribe, or make a purchase with ease.

Embrace responsive design, much like a flexible structure that adapts gracefully to any screen size. Ensure your virtual oasis remains accessible and enjoyable, whether on desktop, tablet, or smartphone.

Lastly, like a benevolent guide, test your website rigorously to identify and resolve any navigational hurdles. Conduct user testing, gather feedback, and refine your design iteratively, ensuring your visitors' pilgrimage is devoid of frustration.

By combining the art of empathy with the precision of a well-crafted architecture, you shall erect a user-friendly interface and seamless navigation for your website. Your digital marketing sanctuary will not only attract visitors but also inspire them to embark on an enriching and memorable journey.

Creating Persuasive Landing Pages And Effective Calls-To-Action

Crafting persuasive landing pages and compelling calls to action for your digital marketing website is akin to composing an enchanting symphony that captivates the hearts of your audience, leading them to take the desired actions like dancers swayed by a mesmerizing melody.

Compose your landing pages with a harmonious blend of clarity and relevance, like the conductor weaving distinct instruments to create a captivating melody. Present a clear value proposition, expressing the benefits of your offerings in a language that resonates with your audience's desires and aspirations.

Design your landing pages with elegance and simplicity, akin to graceful movements that charm the eyes and soothe the soul. Utilize striking visuals, complementing the narrative with compelling images that evoke emotions and reinforce your message.

Introduce your calls to action like a crescendo building to a climactic moment, demanding attention and stirring excitement. Use persuasive language, highlighting the urgency or exclusivity of your offerings to instill a sense of desire and prompt immediate action.

Ensure your calls to action stand out like a powerful soloist amid a symphony, drawing the spotlight to their significance. Use contrasting colors, bold fonts, and strategic placement to make them impossible to ignore.

Harmonize your calls to action with the content of your landing pages, creating a seamless transition that feels like a natural extension of the melody. Align the tone and messaging to maintain the symphonic flow and foster a sense of trust.

Measure the tempo of your performance with A/B testing, refining your landing pages and calls to action iteratively like a musician tuning their instrument. Analyze data and listen to the feedback of your audience, allowing you to fine-tune the symphony to perfection.

With skillful composition and orchestration, your landing pages will entice visitors like an enchanting melody, leading them to dance gracefully with your calls to action. The symphony of persuasion you create shall resonate deeply, leaving a lasting impact on your digital marketing efforts.

* * *

CHAPTER 3: MASTERING SEARCH ENGINE OPTIMIZATION (SEO)

Unveiling The Secrets Of Organic Search Rankings

Unveiling the secrets of organic search rankings for your digital marketing website is akin to embarking on a thrilling quest to uncover hidden treasures in a vast and mysterious landscape. Picture yourself as an intrepid explorer, equipped with curiosity and perseverance, ready to decode the enigmatic algorithms that govern search engines.

Set forth on your expedition armed with the power of keyword research, as though it were a precious map revealing the terrain of user intent. Unearth valuable keywords and phrases that align with your content and resonate with your audience's quest for knowledge.

Navigate through the dense forest of on-page optimization, skillfully treading the path of meta tags, content structure, and internal linking. Forge a clear and engaging path for search engine crawlers to follow, leading them towards the heart of your website.

Venture into the uncharted territory of backlink acquisition, as though you were forging alliances with fellow explorers who vouch for your expertise.

Earn high-quality backlinks from authoritative sources, proving your website's credibility and relevance to the digital world.

Embrace the power of content creation, like a storyteller spinning captivating tales that captivate and delight. Craft valuable and comprehensive content that answers the questions and quenches the thirst of your audience, elevating your digital kingdom to new heights.

Strengthen your fortress of technical SEO, like an architect fortifying the walls of a grand castle. Ensure your website's structure is secure, fast, and accessible, fending off potential obstacles that could hinder your ascent in search rankings.

Explore the shifting sands of search engine updates, for the digital landscape is ever-changing. Stay vigilant and adaptable, adjusting your strategies as you navigate through the evolving algorithms to maintain a competitive edge.

As you uncover the secrets of organic search rankings, remember that the journey itself is as valuable as the destination. Embrace continuous learning and experimentation, and allow your passion for discovery to guide you. With each revelation, your digital marketing website shall emerge as a shining beacon, drawing in a curious and captivated audience from across the digital realm.

Conducting Keyword Research And On-Page Optimization

For conducting keyword research and on-page optimization for your digital marketing website, here are some effective steps to follow:

1. **Keyword Research**:
   - Start by brainstorming relevant topics related to your digital marketing services.

   - Use keyword research tools like Google Keyword Planner, SEMrush, or Ahrefs to find relevant keywords and phrases with search volume and low competition.

   - Focus on long-tail keywords (phrases with three or more words) that are specific and targeted to your services.

2. **Competitor Analysis**:

   - Analyze your competitors' websites to identify the keywords they are ranking for and incorporating in their content.

   - Look for gaps in their content strategy and find opportunities to cover topics they might have missed.

3. **Content Creation**:

   - Create high-quality, informative, and valuable content based on the keywords you've identified. This can include blog posts, articles, guides, and more.

   - Use the keywords naturally in your content, keeping it relevant and user-friendly.

4. **On-Page Optimization**:

   - Optimize your website's meta tags, including title tags and meta descriptions, to include your target keywords.

   - Ensure your content is well-structured with appropriate headers (H1, H2, etc.) and relevant keywords used in them.

- Use descriptive URLs that incorporate your target keywords.

5. **Internal Linking**:

   - Implement internal linking within your content to direct users to other relevant pages on your website.

   - Ensure anchor text (the linked text) is relevant and descriptive.

6. **Page Speed and Mobile Optimization**:

   - Optimize your website for fast loading speed to improve user experience and search engine rankings.

   - Ensure your website is mobile-friendly as more searches are conducted on mobile devices.

7. **Schema Markup**:

   - Implement schema markup on your website to provide search engines with more context about your content, increasing the chances of featured snippets or rich search results.

8. **Regular Updates and Monitoring**:

   - Keep your content fresh and up-to-date to maintain its relevance and authority.

   - Monitor your website's performance and keyword rankings regularly to make necessary adjustments.

Remember that SEO is an ongoing process, and it may take time to see significant results. Be patient and consistent in your efforts, and you should see improvements in your website's visibility and search engine rankings.

Enhancing Website Performance And Mobile Optimization

Elevating your website's performance and optimizing it for mobile devices is akin to fine-tuning the engines of a high-speed racing car, preparing it to race ahead in the fast-paced digital world. Picture yourself as a skilled mechanic, equipped with cutting-edge tools and a passion for excellence, ready to enhance your digital marketing website's performance.

Start by conducting a thorough performance audit, inspecting every component of your website's engine. Optimize images and multimedia files, ensuring they are compressed without compromising quality, reducing loading times like a well-oiled machine firing on all cylinders.

Fine-tune your website's code and scripts, like a precision engineer adjusting the gears for optimal efficiency. Minify CSS and JavaScript files, removing unnecessary elements that might slow down your digital vehicle on its mobile journey.

Integrate caching mechanisms into your website's architecture, creating a smooth and seamless user experience that rivals the acceleration of a racecar. Employ browser caching and leverage Content Delivery Networks (CDNs) to deliver content swiftly to users across the digital racetrack.

Embrace responsive web design like a streamlined chassis, allowing your website to gracefully adapt to various mobile devices, from smartphones to tablets. Ensure that every part of your digital vehicle aligns seamlessly, offering a consistent and captivating experience to users, regardless of the device they use.

Invest in mobile-first design, placing mobile optimization at the forefront of your digital engineering process. Prioritize the essentials, keeping your website lean and agile on smaller screens, propelling it forward to surpass competitors and secure a pole position in mobile search rankings.

Continuously test your website's performance on different devices, using a range of tools and emulators, just as a skilled mechanic conducts rigorous testing before a race. Monitor loading times, interactions, and responsiveness, making timely adjustments to keep your digital marketing website at peak performance.

With precision engineering and an unwavering focus on mobile optimization, your digital marketing website will become a powerful contender on the digital racetrack, accelerating past competitors and delivering an unrivaled user experience. Just as a finely-tuned racing car leaves its rivals in the dust, your website will leave a lasting impression on users, ensuring they return for more exhilarating interactions on your optimized digital racetrack.

* * *

CHAPTER 4: DOMINATING PAID ADVERTISING AND PPC

Utilizing Pay-Per-Click (PPC) Campaigns Effectively

Harnessing the power of pay-per-click (PPC) campaigns for your digital marketing website is akin to wielding a finely crafted sword in a strategic battle, cutting through the noise to claim victory in the competitive digital arena. Picture yourself as a seasoned warrior, armed with insight and precision, ready to conquer the realm of PPC and emerge triumphant.

Begin by honing your target audience like a skilled archer, aiming your PPC campaigns directly at those most likely to engage with your offerings. Laser-focus your keywords and demographics, ensuring every click carries the potential for conversion, like a well-aimed arrow striking the heart of your audience.

Arm your campaigns with captivating ad copy, as though crafting a powerful battle cry that resonates with your audience's desires and aspirations. Use persuasive language and unique selling propositions to inspire action, drawing users to your digital fortress with irresistible allure.

Deploy A/B testing as your shield, gathering valuable data like a shield deflecting enemy attacks. Continuously experiment with ad variations, landing page designs, and calls-to-action, optimizing your campaigns to withstand the ever-evolving battlefield of digital marketing.

Fortify your PPC campaigns with robust tracking and analytics, like a vigilant scout gathering intelligence on the movements of your adversaries. Measure key performance metrics, monitor click-through rates, and analyze conversion data to inform your strategy, empowering you to make informed decisions that outmaneuver competitors.

Allocate your budget strategically, distributing resources like a wise general deploying troops with precision. Optimize bids, control spend, and invest in high-performing campaigns, ensuring you maximize your return on investment and maintain a strong position on the battlefield.

Embrace remarketing as your secret weapon, engaging with previous visitors who are just a step away from conversion. Target them with tailored messages, rekindling their interest and bringing them back to your digital encampment, ready to take the final leap.

With a well-crafted PPC strategy and a warrior's spirit, your digital marketing website will emerge victorious in the battlefield of pay-per-click campaigns. Just as a skilled commander leads their troops to triumph, you shall conquer the digital landscape, gaining visibility, driving conversions, and securing a dominant position amidst the chaos of the competitive digital realm.

Maximizing ROI Through Keyword Targeting And Bid Management

Maximizing return on investment (ROI) through keyword targeting and bid management for your digital marketing website is akin to orchestrating a symphony of precision and harmony, where each note played contributes to a grand crescendo of success. Picture yourself as a

skilled conductor, guiding your campaign with finesse and artistry, optimizing every element to achieve optimal performance.
Start by meticulously selecting your keywords, as though curating a collection of musical instruments that harmonize perfectly. Conduct thorough keyword research to identify high-impact terms that align with your goals and resonate with your audience's search intent.

Fine-tune your bid management like a maestro adjusting the tempo of a symphony, optimizing bids strategically to ensure cost-effectiveness and optimal exposure. Leverage data-driven insights to set competitive bids, allowing your digital marketing symphony to reach the right audience at the right moment.

Adopt a granular approach to keyword targeting, segmenting your campaigns like a master composer crafting distinct movements. Group keywords based on relevance, and tailor ad copy and landing pages accordingly, providing a personalized experience for your audience that strikes a harmonious chord.

Monitor your campaign performance with acute attention to detail, much like a conductor listening attentively to every note played by the orchestra. Analyze data, track conversions, and measure ROI, enabling you to fine-tune your strategy, refining each aspect for maximum impact.

Embrace the art of negative keyword management, acting as a vigilant guardian of your budget, much like a conductor protecting the symphony from discordant sounds. Eliminate irrelevant search queries that drain resources, allowing your campaign to resonate with precision and efficiency.
Continuously optimize and experiment, like a composer composing a symphony that evolves with each performance. Test different bidding strategies, explore new keyword opportunities, and adapt your tactics to navigate the ever-changing landscape of digital marketing.

By conducting your keyword targeting and bid management symphony with mastery and finesse, your digital marketing website shall resonate with exceptional ROI, delivering a symphony of success that captivates your audience and leaves a lasting impact in the digital realm.

Mastering Ad Copywriting And Split Testing For Optimal Results

To master the art of ad copywriting and split testing for optimal results in your digital marketing website is akin to refining your skills as a virtuoso pianist, coaxing melodies that captivate your audience and leaving them yearning for more. Picture yourself as a wordsmith conductor, skillfully crafting harmonies of persuasive language and conducting experiments that fine-tune your compositions to perfection.

Start by understanding the rhythm of your target audience, as a pianist feels the pulse of the music before striking the keys. Dive into market research to unearth the desires and pain points of your audience, allowing you to compose ad copy that resonates deeply with their needs.
Craft compelling ad copy like a composer weaving intricate melodies, capturing attention and evoking emotions in a few concise lines. Embrace the power of storytelling, painting vivid narratives that draw your audience into your digital symphony, inspiring them to take action.

Emphasize the crescendo of your unique selling propositions, like a pianist showcasing their virtuosity in a thrilling performance. Highlight the benefits of your offerings, standing out amidst the digital noise, and captivating your audience's attention with irresistible allure.

With your ad copy ready, embrace the symphony of split testing, akin to a pianist refining their technique through countless practice sessions. Create variations of your ad copy and experiment with different headlines, calls-to-action, and visuals, testing their impact on click-through rates and conversions.

Analyze the results of your split tests with precision, like a conductor studying the nuances of each performance. Uncover valuable insights, identifying winning ad copies that strike a chord with your audience and refining those that need improvement.

Continuously iterate and refine your ad copy, embracing a virtuoso mindset that pursues excellence through relentless practice and adaptation. Strive to surpass your previous best, refining your compositions and split testing strategies to achieve optimal results that resonate harmoniously with your digital marketing website.

Just as a virtuoso pianist enchants their audience with their mastery, your ad copywriting and split testing prowess shall elevate your digital marketing website to new heights, captivating visitors and orchestrating a symphony of success that resonates deeply, leaving a lasting impact in the digital realm.

* * *

CHAPTER 5: HARNESSING THE POWER OF SOCIAL MEDIA MARKETING

Creating A Social Media Strategy Aligned With Your Goals

Crafting a personalized social media strategy aligned with your personal goals for digital marketing is akin to sculpting a masterpiece that reflects your unique identity and resonates deeply with your audience. Picture yourself as an artist, with a blank canvas of social platforms awaiting your creative strokes.

Start by defining your personal goals as the foundation of your artistic vision. Understand what you wish to achieve through your digital marketing efforts, whether it's building brand awareness, driving website traffic, increasing engagement, or generating leads.

Paint a clear picture of your target audience, as though sketching the outlines of your ideal spectators. Delve into their preferences, interests, and pain points, understanding what captivates and compels them to engage with your content.

Choose the right social media platforms as your color palette, selecting those that align with your goals and resonate with your audience. If your target audience prefers visual content, platforms like Instagram and

Pinterest might be ideal, while LinkedIn might suit a more professional focus.

Craft your content with a unique and authentic voice, like an artist infusing their paintings with a signature style. Share valuable insights, engaging stories, and meaningful interactions, creating a compelling narrative that reflects your personal brand and leaves a lasting impression on your audience.

Embrace consistency as your guiding principle, like a steady hand tracing the contours of your masterpiece. Establish a content calendar and maintain regular posting schedules to build trust and loyalty with your audience.

Integrate a variety of content types, like blending different brushstrokes to create a diverse and engaging canvas. Combine visuals, videos, infographics, and written posts, offering a well-rounded experience that keeps your audience captivated and coming back for more.

Measure your progress like an observant art critic, analyzing data and feedback to gauge the impact of your social media strategy. Adjust your approach accordingly, learning from your successes and challenges to continuously refine and improve your digital marketing artwork.

In the end, your social media strategy will be a true reflection of your personal goals and identity as an artist. As you wield your digital paintbrush, your masterpiece will unfold, resonating deeply with your audience, and leaving an indelible mark in the digital art gallery.

Engaging And Growing Your Audience On Various Platforms

Captivating and cultivating your audience on social media platforms for digital marketing is akin to nurturing a vibrant garden of connections, where each seed of engagement blossoms into a flourishing community. Picture yourself as a dedicated gardener, tending to the needs of your audience with care and creativity, fostering a space where growth and interaction thrive.

1. Sow the Seeds of Value: Plant the seeds of valuable content that enrich your audience's digital landscape. Cultivate a diverse garden of posts, including educational pieces, entertaining stories, and thought-provoking insights. Nurture your content with authenticity and relevance, nurturing a loyal following that finds value in your digital oasis.

2. Water with Consistent Presence: Tend to your garden regularly with consistent and active presence. Water your social media platforms with frequent engagement, responding to comments, messages, and mentions promptly. Your attentive care will foster trust and foster a sense of community among your audience.

3. Fertilize with Visual Appeal: Enrich your garden with eye-catching visuals that bloom like vibrant flowers in the digital realm. Utilize high-quality images, videos, and graphics that captivate attention and evoke emotions, drawing visitors to explore your virtual garden further.

4. Prune for Quality: Trim away clutter and unnecessary noise, like a gardener removing weeds that hinder growth. Focus on delivering quality content rather than overwhelming your audience with quantity. Prune your content strategy to emphasize substance over saturation.

5. Cultivate Connection: Engage with your audience genuinely, like a gardener forging bonds with each plant in their care. Participate in conversations, ask questions, and actively listen to feedback. Cultivate connections through meaningful interactions that build rapport and trust.

6. Cross-Pollinate with Collaboration: Seek opportunities for cross-platform collaborations and partnerships, like a gardener introducing complementary

species. Collaborating with influencers or like-minded brands can expose your garden to new audiences, fostering organic growth.

7. Harvest User-Generated Content: Harvest the fruits of your audience's creativity by encouraging user-generated content. Run contests or campaigns that inspire users to share their experiences with your brand, turning them into active participants in your digital garden.

8. Foster Growth with Influencers: Invite influencers to your garden to share their expertise and insights. Their presence can act as a catalyst for growth, attracting new visitors and followers who are drawn to their authority and influence.

9. Adapt and Evolve: Remain adaptive and open to change, like a gardener adjusting their strategies based on weather and seasons. Monitor trends, stay informed about platform updates, and be willing to evolve your approach to maintain a thriving digital garden.

By nurturing your audience with the love and dedication of a skilled gardener, your social media platforms will flourish with engaged followers, cultivating a vibrant community that reaps the rewards of your digital marketing efforts. Just as a garden brings joy to its caretaker, your flourishing audience will bring fulfillment and success to your digital marketing endeavors.

Leveraging Social Media Analytics For Data-Driven Decision-Making

Leveraging social media analytics for data-driven decision-making in your social media marketing is akin to equipping yourself with a powerful telescope, peering into the vast universe of user insights to navigate your digital course with precision and purpose.

1. Set Clear Objectives: Define your social media marketing goals and align them with your overall business objectives. Whether it's increasing brand awareness, driving website traffic, or boosting engagement, having clear objectives will guide your data analysis and decision-making process.

2. Track Key Performance Metrics: Identify the key performance indicators (KPIs) relevant to your objectives. Metrics such as reach, engagement, click-through rates, conversion rates, and follower growth are essential to measure the impact of your social media efforts.

3. Utilize Social Media Insights: Each platform provides its own analytics tools that offer valuable data on audience demographics, post performance, and engagement metrics. Dive into these insights regularly to gain a deeper understanding of your audience's behavior and preferences.

4. Aggregate Data from Multiple Sources: Integrate data from various social media platforms and other analytics tools to form a comprehensive view of your social media performance. Using data aggregation tools can streamline this process and provide a more holistic perspective.

5. Analyze Trends and Patterns: Identify trends and patterns in your data to spot opportunities and challenges. Look for content types, posting times, or specific topics that resonate well with your audience and leverage these insights to refine your content strategy.

6. Benchmark Against Competitors: Monitor your competitors' social media performance and benchmark your metrics against theirs. This competitive analysis can reveal areas where you excel and areas that need improvement, guiding your decision-making process.

7. A/B Test and Experiment: Conduct A/B tests to compare the performance of different content formats, visuals, copy variations, and posting schedules.

These experiments provide valuable data on what resonates best with your audience and inform future content strategies.

8. Monitor Campaign Performance: Measure the success of your social media campaigns and promotions using tracking parameters and URL tagging. This data will enable you to assess the ROI of specific initiatives and allocate resources effectively.

9. Make Data-Driven Adjustments: Based on your social media analytics, make informed decisions and adjustments to your content strategy, posting frequency, targeting options, and ad spend. Continuously optimize your approach to improve results.

10. Create Regular Reports: Develop regular reports and dashboards to present your social media insights in a visually engaging and actionable format. Regular reporting facilitates communication with stakeholders and supports evidence-based decision-making.

By harnessing the power of social media analytics, you transform raw data into actionable insights that fuel your social media marketing strategies. Just as an experienced navigator relies on precise instruments, your data-driven decisions will guide your social media journey towards success, enabling you to engage and resonate with your audience with greater impact and effectiveness.

* * *

CHAPTER 6: CULTIVATING CONTENT MARKETING EXCELLENCE

Crafting Compelling And Shareable Content Across Channels

Crafting compelling and shareable content across channels for your digital market is akin to preparing a delectable feast that tantalizes the taste buds and leaves guests eager to share their culinary delight. Picture yourself as a master chef, skillfully combining ingredients of creativity and strategy to create a feast for the senses.

1. Understand Your Audience's Palate: Begin by studying the preferences and cravings of your target audience, like a chef observing their guests' culinary preferences. Uncover what topics, formats, and storytelling styles resonate with them, tailoring your content to satisfy their appetites.

2. Season with Storytelling: Infuse your content with storytelling, like adding aromatic spices that elevate flavors. Weave narratives that captivate emotions, immerse your audience in relatable experiences, and connect them with your brand on a deeper level.

3. Serve a Variety of Formats: Offer a diverse menu of content formats, appealing to different tastes like a chef presenting an array of dishes. Mix

up blogs, videos, infographics, and interactive content to keep your audience engaged and eager for more.

4. Garnish with Visual Appeal: Enhance your content's visual appeal, much like a chef garnishing a dish with colorful accents. Utilize eye-catching images, graphics, and videos that entice your audience to take a closer look and share with their networks.

5. Sprinkle in Humor and Wit: Add a dash of humor and wit to your content, like a chef adding a pinch of spice for an unexpected kick. Humorous content is highly shareable and fosters a positive association with your brand.

6. Use Emotion as the Main Ingredient: Stir emotions in your audience like a chef stirring flavors in a pot. Create content that evokes joy, surprise, inspiration, or empathy, forging emotional connections that compel them to share with others.

7. Plate Your Content for Readability: Present your content in a visually appealing and easy-to-digest manner, just as a chef artfully plates their culinary creation. Use clear headings, bullet points, and concise language to make your content easily scannable and shareable.

8. Invite Participation and Interaction: Encourage audience participation, as a chef invites diners to customize their meal. Include polls, quizzes, or calls-to-action that prompt engagement and sharing, transforming your audience into active participants in your digital feast.

9. Pair with Timely and Trending Topics: Stay updated on the latest trends and current events, like a chef incorporating seasonal ingredients for a timely menu. Tap into trending topics, relevant hashtags, and real-time conversations to ensure your content remains relevant and share-worthy.

10. Taste Test and Refine: Like a chef who tastes and adjusts their dish, continually evaluate the performance of your content across channels. Analyze engagement metrics, feedback, and shares to refine your content

strategy, ensuring it continues to satisfy your audience's appetite for valuable and shareable content.

By crafting content that tantalizes the senses and nourishes the interests of your audience, your digital feast will become a sought-after culinary experience that leaves a lasting impression and sparks a desire to share the delightful flavors of your brand with others.

Implementing Effective Storytelling And Brand Narratives

Implementing effective storytelling and brand narratives for your digital marketing business is akin to penning a captivating novel that enthralls readers, immersing them in a world of emotions and connections. Picture yourself as a skilled wordsmith, weaving a tapestry of narratives that leave an indelible mark on your audience's hearts and minds.

1. Unveil Your Origin Story: Begin with the prologue of your brand's origin story, narrating the journey that brought your business into existence. Paint a vivid picture of your vision, struggles, and triumphs, drawing your audience into the narrative with authenticity and relatability.

2. Enchant with Characters: Introduce compelling characters that personify your brand's values and personality. Whether it's your founders, employees, or satisfied customers, humanize your brand through their stories, making your audience emotionally invested in your digital marketing adventure.

3. Craft an Engaging Plot: Develop a compelling plot that drives your brand narrative forward, much like a novelist crafting twists and turns that keep readers eager for the next chapter. Align your brand's milestones, product launches, and achievements with the unfolding story, building anticipation and interest.

4. Evoke Emotions with Conflict and Resolution: Introduce conflict and challenges that your audience can relate to, sparking empathy and emotional connections. Demonstrate how your brand's solutions and products resolve these conflicts, leaving a lasting impression on your audience's emotions.

5. Create a Consistent Tone and Voice: Establish a consistent tone and voice for your brand, much like a novelist maintaining a cohesive narrative style. Whether it's humor, compassion, or authority, infuse your storytelling with a distinct voice that reinforces your brand's identity.

6. Utilize Visual Imagery: Paint a vivid picture with visual imagery that complements your narrative, akin to an author evoking scenes through descriptive language. Utilize high-quality images, videos, and graphics that amplify the emotional impact of your storytelling.

7. Engage Across Multiple Channels: Extend your narrative across various digital channels, just as an author shares their story through different mediums. Tailor your storytelling to suit each platform, ensuring your brand narrative reaches a diverse audience.

8. Encourage Audience Participation: Turn your audience into active participants in your brand narrative, like an interactive novel that allows readers to shape the story's outcome. Encourage user-generated content, testimonials, and feedback, fostering a sense of community and ownership.

9. Evoke Curiosity and Anticipation: Leave your audience craving for the next chapter of your brand's narrative, much like an author's cliffhanger ending that keeps readers eagerly anticipating the sequel. Tease upcoming developments and product launches to maintain intrigue and engagement.

10. Measure Impact and Refine: Analyze the impact of your storytelling efforts through engagement metrics, customer feedback, and brand sentiment analysis. Continuously refine your storytelling strategy based on

insights, ensuring your digital marketing business's narrative evolves with the changing needs of your audience.

With the pen of effective storytelling and brand narratives in your hand, your digital marketing business will create a literary masterpiece that captivates and resonates with your audience. Like a timeless novel that stands the test of time, your brand narrative will endure, forging lasting connections that span the pages of your digital journey.

Measuring Content Performance And Adapting Strategies Accordingly

Measuring content performance and adapting strategies accordingly for your digital marketing is akin to conducting a symphony, where each note is meticulously analyzed to fine-tune the harmony of your digital composition. Picture yourself as a discerning conductor, guiding your content with precision and insight to create a captivating masterpiece.

1. Set Clear Objectives as Your Baton: Begin by setting clear objectives as your guiding baton, directing the performance of your content. Align your goals with your business objectives, whether it's increasing website traffic, lead generation, or enhancing brand awareness.

2. Conduct a Content Audit Like a Maestro's Rehearsal: Commence your performance with a content audit, much like a maestro's rehearsal, assessing the impact of your existing content. Identify top-performing pieces, analyze engagement metrics, and identify gaps or areas for improvement.

3. Measure Key Performance Metrics as Your Sheet Music: Use key performance metrics as your sheet music, guiding your content's performance. Track metrics such as click-through rates, time on page, bounce rates, and conversion rates to gauge content effectiveness.

4. Segment Your Audience Like a Scored Symphony: Segment your audience, like sections in a scored symphony, to understand their preferences and behavior better. Analyze data on demographics, interests, and behaviors to tailor your content for maximum resonance.

5. Harmonize Content with Customer Journey Stages: Align your content with the customer journey stages, like notes in harmony, addressing different needs and pain points. Craft content for awareness, consideration, and decision stages to nurture prospects effectively.

6. A/B Testing as Your Melodic Variation: Conduct A/B testing as your melodic variation, experimenting with different content elements to discover what resonates best. Test headlines, visuals, CTAs, and content formats, and let the data guide your direction.

7. Embrace Social Listening as Your Audience Applause: Embrace social listening, akin to listening to the audience applause, to understand sentiment and gather feedback. Monitor mentions, comments, and conversations to adapt your content to meet your audience's desires.

8. Analyze Website Analytics for Performance Ensemble: Utilize website analytics as your performance ensemble, studying how content influences user behavior. Analyze navigation paths, session duration, and conversion funnels to optimize content placement and engagement.

9. Refine Content with Iterative Improvisation: Continuously refine your content strategy with iterative improvisation, like a musician perfecting their technique. Implement insights from data analysis, audience feedback, and market trends to evolve and enhance your content over time.

10. Create Performance Reports as Your Encore: Present content performance reports as your encore, showcasing the impact of your digital symphony. Craft visually appealing and actionable reports to communicate insights to stakeholders, guiding future content strategies.

By measuring content performance with the precision of a conductor's baton, your digital marketing efforts will create a harmonious ensemble that captivates and resonates with your audience. Like a symphony that evolves with each performance, your content strategies will adapt and flourish, ensuring your digital composition continues to strike the right chords and delight audiences on the digital stage.

* * *

CHAPTER 7: EMAIL MARKETING AND AUTOMATION

Building An Email List And Segmenting Your Audience

Building an email list and segmenting your audience for digital marketing is akin to crafting a personalized library of cherished books, where each volume speaks directly to the interests and preferences of its reader. Picture yourself as a literary curator, carefully selecting and organizing content to create a meaningful and engaging collection.

1. Create Compelling Opt-In Incentives: Begin by offering valuable opt-in incentives, like exclusive literary treasures, that entice visitors to join your email library. E-books, guides, discounts, or access to insider content act as alluring invitations for audience members to subscribe.

2. Design Captivating Sign-Up Forms: Craft sign-up forms that act as welcoming book covers, capturing attention with eye-catching visuals and persuasive copy. Make them easily accessible on your website and across digital touchpoints to encourage subscriptions.

3. Personalize Your Welcome Series: Once readers step into your library, welcome them with a personalized series of emails, like a warm greeting

from a knowledgeable librarian. Tailor the content based on their interests and behavior, nurturing the beginnings of a meaningful connection.

4. Segment Your Audience into Literary Genres: Segment your email list into distinct literary genres, grouping subscribers based on their preferences and interactions. Analyze data such as past purchases, content engagement, or demographics to categorize your readers effectively.

5. Craft Tailored Content for Each Segment: Like curating customized reading lists, create content that speaks directly to each audience segment's interests. Send targeted promotions, relevant blog articles, or personalized product recommendations to enhance engagement.

6. Leverage Behavioral Triggers as Plot Twists: Utilize behavioral triggers like plot twists, activating automated email sequences based on user actions. Set triggers for abandoned carts, content downloads, or website visits to deliver timely and contextually relevant messages.

7. Encourage Two-Way Communication: Foster a dialogue with your readers, as a librarian engages in insightful book discussions. Encourage feedback, conduct surveys, or prompt replies to learn more about their preferences and refine your literary offerings.

8. Optimize for Mobile Reading Pleasure: Ensure your emails are optimized for mobile devices, delivering a seamless reading experience akin to the comfort of an e-reader. Mobile responsiveness increases engagement and allows readers to enjoy your literary content on-the-go.

9. Keep Your Library Fresh with Exclusive Content: Continuously add exclusive content to your library, like unpublished manuscripts, to entice readers to stay subscribed. Regularly update your subscribers with fresh and relevant material that keeps them eagerly anticipating each new release.

10. Analyze Reading Habits with Insights: Utilize email analytics as your literary insights, observing reader behavior and interactions with your

content. Measure open rates, click-through rates, and conversion data to gauge the impact of your emails and refine your email marketing strategy.

By building an email library and curating personalized literary experiences, your digital marketing efforts will foster lasting relationships with your audience. Just as a curated library leaves readers captivated and coming back for more, your segmented email campaigns will engage and resonate with subscribers, turning them into devoted readers of your digital narrative.

Crafting Personalized And Engaging Email Campaigns

Crafting personalized and engaging email campaigns for your digital marketing is akin to composing a heartfelt letter to a dear friend, where every word carries the warmth of familiarity and every sentence resonates with genuine care. Picture yourself as a thoughtful correspondent, creating email campaigns that foster meaningful connections with your audience.

1. Begin with a Warm Greeting: Open your email campaign with a warm greeting, much like a friendly embrace that sets the tone for your message. Address your recipients by their names, creating an immediate sense of personalization and familiarity.

2. Understand Your Audience's Interests: Dive deep into your audience's interests and preferences, as though reading the chapters of their lives. Segment your email list based on demographics, behavior, and past interactions, tailoring each campaign to specific reader personas.

3. Craft Compelling Subject Lines as Alluring Book Covers: Create subject lines that act as alluring book covers, captivating attention and enticing

readers to open your email. Use personalization, curiosity, or urgency to pique their interest and make your message irresistible.

4. Tell Engaging Stories: Weave engaging stories within your emails, like enthralling tales that captivate your readers' hearts. Share real-life anecdotes, customer success stories, or behind-the-scenes narratives that create an emotional connection and foster brand loyalty.

5. Provide Value with Exclusive Content: Offer exclusive content to your readers, much like sharing treasured secrets between friends. Provide valuable insights, insider tips, or special promotions that make your subscribers feel appreciated and rewarded for their loyalty.

6. Deliver Timely and Relevant Messages: Time your email campaigns strategically, delivering messages that are timely and relevant, like messages arriving at just the right moment. Use behavioral triggers and automation to ensure your emails align with each recipient's journey.
7. Encourage Interaction and Feedback: Like inviting thoughtful conversations, encourage interaction with your email campaigns. Include surveys, polls, or calls-to-action that prompt readers to reply or provide feedback, showing that their voices are valued.

8. Personalize Content and Recommendations: Customize your email content and recommendations, as though handpicking book selections for each reader's taste. Use past purchase history, browsing behavior, and preferences to curate personalized offers and suggestions.

9. Design Visually Appealing Layouts: Design visually appealing email layouts that enhance the reading experience, much like flipping through beautifully designed book pages. Use eye-catching visuals, clear formatting, and mobile responsiveness to keep readers engaged.

10. Express Genuine Gratitude and Acknowledgment: Express genuine gratitude and acknowledgment to your subscribers, just as a correspondent thanks their pen pal for their ongoing connection. Celebrate milestones,

offer special rewards, and show appreciation for their role in your digital journey.

By crafting email campaigns with the sincerity of a heartfelt letter, your digital marketing efforts will foster deep connections with your audience. Like cherished correspondents, your personalized emails will resonate with readers, creating a bond that endures and ensures they eagerly await each new message in your digital exchange.

Implementing Automation And Nurturing Customer Relationships

Implementing automation and nurturing customer relationships for your digital marketing is akin to creating a well-oiled clockwork of thoughtful gestures, where each tick and tock contributes to building lasting connections with your audience. Picture yourself as a meticulous horologist, designing an intricate timepiece that keeps the gears of engagement and loyalty in perfect harmony.

1. Welcome with a Personalized Greeting: Begin by setting the timepiece in motion with a warm and personalized welcome. Implement automated welcome emails that address new subscribers by name and express gratitude for joining your digital journey.

2. Segmentation as Precise Timekeeping: Segment your audience with precision, like fine-tuning the gears of a clock to suit different preferences and needs. Categorize subscribers based on demographics, behavior, and interests to deliver tailored messages.

3. Automate Drip Campaigns as Steady Ticking: Create drip campaigns that operate as steady ticking, delivering a series of timed and relevant messages to nurture prospects. Automate emails that gradually educate, entertain, and build trust with your audience.

4. Use Triggers for Timely Interactions: Employ triggers like a well-calibrated chronometer, initiating automated responses based on user actions or behavior. Set triggers for abandoned carts, downloads, or website visits, delivering timely messages that match the moment.

5. Personalization as Custom Clock Faces: Embrace personalization as custom clock faces, enhancing the appeal of your emails. Address recipients by name, recommend products based on past purchases, and tailor content to match individual interests.

6. Automate Follow-ups and Engagement: Automate follow-up emails and engagement campaigns to maintain a constant connection with your audience. Use reminders, feedback requests, or product updates to keep your brand top-of-mind.

7. Implement Loyalty Programs as Pendulums: Introduce loyalty programs as pendulums, swinging back and forth to reward customer engagement. Implement automated loyalty emails that acknowledge milestones and offer exclusive rewards.

8. Leverage Predictive Analytics as Time Forecasting: Utilize predictive analytics as time forecasting, anticipating customer needs and behavior. Analyze data to anticipate customer preferences and provide proactive recommendations.

9. Automate Re-engagement Strategies as Clockwork Reminders: Implement automated re-engagement strategies, like clockwork reminders, to win back inactive subscribers. Send targeted offers or content to rekindle their interest and encourage them to return.

10. Continuous Monitoring and Adjustments as Timekeeping Maintenance: Continuously monitor your automation efforts and make adjustments as part of timekeeping maintenance. Analyze performance metrics, collect feedback, and refine your automation to optimize customer relationships.

By implementing automation with the precision of a skilled horologist, your digital marketing efforts will nurture customer relationships with impeccable timing. Like a well-crafted timepiece, your automated campaigns will keep the gears of engagement, loyalty, and customer satisfaction turning seamlessly, ensuring your audience's connection with your brand stands the test of time.

* * *

CHAPTER 8: INFLUENCER MARKETING AND PARTNERSHIPS

Identifying And Collaborating With Influential Figures In Your Industry

Identifying and collaborating with influential figures in the digital marketing industry is akin to embarking on an adventurous expedition to discover hidden gems in the vast landscape of professionals. Picture yourself as an intrepid explorer, navigating the digital realm to forge meaningful connections with these influential trailblazers.

1. Conduct Extensive Research as Your Map: Begin your expedition with extensive research as your map, delving into the digital marketing landscape to identify potential influential figures. Look for thought leaders, industry experts, and content creators who resonate with your niche and target audience.

2. Cultivate Genuine Interest as Your Compass: Cultivate genuine interest in the work of these influential figures, as your compass guiding your approach. Engage with their content, follow their social media, and subscribe to their newsletters to understand their perspectives and contributions.

3. Build Authentic Relationships as Your Travel Companions: Forge authentic relationships as your trusted travel companions, connecting with these influencers on a human level. Engage in meaningful conversations, offer thoughtful insights, and show appreciation for their expertise.

4. Leverage Social Media as Your Communication Beacon: Utilize social media as your communication beacon, reaching out to influencers through direct messages or mentions. Share their content, tag them in relevant posts, and participate in discussions to catch their attention.

5. Offer Value as Your Currency: Offer value as your currency to cultivate reciprocity with these influential figures. Provide helpful resources, collaborate on co-created content, or share insights that align with their interests and objectives.

6. Attend Virtual Events and Webinars as Your Expedition Grounds: Participate in virtual events, webinars, and industry conferences as your expedition grounds, where you can interact with influential figures. Pose thoughtful questions, join discussions, and network with attendees to expand your connections.

7. Create Shareable and Relevant Content as Your Discovery Trophies: Produce shareable and relevant content as your discovery trophies, showcasing your expertise and thought leadership. Influencers are more likely to collaborate with those who produce valuable and engaging content.

8. Offer Guest Contributions as Your Collaboration Request: Extend guest contribution offers as your collaboration request, inviting influencers to contribute to your blog, podcast, or webinar series. This mutually beneficial arrangement expands their reach while boosting your credibility.

9. Leverage Influencer Marketing Platforms as Your Discovery Tools: Explore influencer marketing platforms as your discovery tools, connecting you with influencers seeking collaboration opportunities. These platforms facilitate a streamlined approach to identify and engage potential partners.

10. Practice Patience and Persistence as Your Enduring Spirit: Remember that building relationships with influential figures takes time, so practice patience and persistence as your enduring spirit. Stay committed to your authentic approach, and let connections develop organically over time.

By embarking on this expedition with curiosity, authenticity, and perseverance, you will navigate the digital marketing landscape, discovering and collaborating with influential figures who elevate your brand's visibility and credibility. Like an explorer unearthing hidden treasures, your collaboration efforts will uncover exciting opportunities that propel your digital marketing endeavors to new heights.

Developing Mutually Beneficial Partnerships And Sponsorships

Developing mutually beneficial partnerships and sponsorships for your digital marketing is akin to orchestrating a harmonious duet, where both parties play distinct notes that blend seamlessly into a beautiful composition. Picture yourself as a skilled conductor, orchestrating collaborations that resonate with authenticity and drive collective success.

1. Identify Complementary Players: Begin by identifying complementary players, much like a conductor selecting musicians with compatible talents. Look for brands, influencers, or organizations that share your values, target audience, and goals for a strong partnership foundation.

2. Align Objectives as Your Melodic Score: Align your objectives with your potential partner's objectives, like a melodic score that guides your collaborative performance. Ensure shared goals and mutual benefits, fostering a clear understanding of the collective vision.

3. Create Unique Value Propositions: Craft unique value propositions for each collaboration, akin to composing harmonies that highlight individual strengths. Showcase the specific advantages and opportunities that your partnership offers to entice potential sponsors.

4. Establish Clear Expectations as Your Musical Notes: Set clear expectations as your musical notes, outlining each party's responsibilities and deliverables. Define roles, timelines, and key performance indicators to ensure a harmonious and well-coordinated collaboration.

5. Leverage Authentic Relationships: Build authentic relationships with potential partners, just as a conductor fosters a deep connection with musicians. Engage in meaningful conversations, demonstrate genuine interest, and show how the collaboration aligns with their brand vision.

6. Offer Valuable Incentives as Your Crescendo: Provide valuable incentives as your crescendo, enhancing the appeal of the partnership. Offer promotional opportunities, access to your audience, or exclusive benefits that entice potential sponsors to join your digital symphony.

7. Collaborate on Co-Created Content as Your Duet: Engage in co-creation of content as your duet, producing collaborative pieces that blend both brand's voices. Partner on webinars, eBooks, or social media campaigns to leverage combined expertise and reach.

8. Amplify Each Other's Reach as Your Symphony: Amplify each other's reach as your symphony, leveraging the power of cross-promotion. Share each other's content, collaborate on events, and mention partners in newsletters to broaden your digital audience.

9. Measure and Celebrate Success as Your Applause: Measure the impact of your partnerships and celebrate successes together, like the applause after a well-received performance. Analyze performance metrics, assess ROI, and recognize achievements to foster a strong, lasting bond.

10. Nurture Long-Term Relationships as Your Ongoing Concerto: Treat partnerships as an ongoing concerto, nurturing long-term collaborations beyond a one-time performance. Cultivate strong relationships, continuously innovate, and explore new opportunities to evolve and grow together.

By conducting your partnerships with authenticity, alignment, and shared goals, your digital marketing symphony will resonate with harmonious collaborations that elevate both brands. Like a conductor leading a compelling duet, your mutually beneficial partnerships and sponsorships will create a harmonious masterpiece that leaves a lasting impression on your audience and strengthens your digital marketing efforts.

Measuring The Impact And ROI Of Influencer Marketing Efforts

Measuring the impact and ROI of influencer marketing efforts for your digital marketing is akin to conducting an analytical symphony, where data and insights harmonize to reveal the true resonance of your collaboration. Picture yourself as a discerning conductor, orchestrating a performance of metrics and analytics to evaluate the effectiveness of your influencer partnerships.

1. Set Clear Objectives as Your Musical Score: Begin by setting clear objectives as your musical score, guiding the direction of your influencer marketing campaign. Define specific goals such as brand awareness, website traffic, lead generation, or sales to form the foundation of your measurement strategy.

2. Track Key Performance Indicators (KPIs) as Your Melodic Notes: Track key performance indicators (KPIs) as your melodic notes, capturing essential data points to assess your campaign's impact. Measure metrics like reach, engagement, clicks, conversions, and revenue to gauge the success of each collaboration.

3. Utilize Unique Tracking Links as Your Harmonious Chords: Implement unique tracking links as your harmonious chords, enabling you to attribute specific actions to each influencer's efforts. These links help monitor traffic and conversions driven by individual influencers, providing valuable insights.

4. Analyze Audience Engagement as Your Crescendo: Analyze audience engagement as your crescendo, evaluating the level of interaction and resonance between influencers' content and your target audience. Assess comments, likes, shares, and sentiment to understand the impact of influencer-generated content.

5. Measure Conversion Rates as Your Rhythmic Tempo: Measure conversion rates as your rhythmic tempo, indicating how effectively influencer campaigns lead to desired actions. Analyze the conversion funnel, from awareness to purchase, to identify which influencers drive higher conversions.

6. Assess Brand Mentions and Sentiment as Your Melodic Harmony: Assess brand mentions and sentiment as your melodic harmony, evaluating the perception of your brand among the influencer's audience. Monitor brand mentions in posts and conversations to understand the sentiment generated by the collaboration.

7. Compare Cost vs. Revenue as Your Performance Ensemble: Compare the cost of influencer collaborations with the revenue generated as your performance ensemble. Calculate ROI by analyzing the investment made in each campaign against the sales or leads attributed to influencer-driven efforts.

8. Conduct A/B Tests as Your Variations in Sound: Conduct A/B tests as your variations in sound, experimenting with different influencer strategies or content formats. Compare the results to identify what approaches yield the most impactful and cost-effective outcomes.

9. Leverage Influencer Marketing Platforms as Your Orchestra: Utilize influencer marketing platforms as your orchestra, centralizing data and providing performance insights. These platforms help streamline influencer collaboration management and offer comprehensive metrics for evaluation.

10. Seek Feedback and Iteratively Improve as Your Ongoing Symphony: Seek feedback from influencers and your internal team, like an ongoing symphony of improvement. Continuously refine your influencer marketing strategy based on insights, learning from both successes and challenges to optimize future campaigns.

By conducting this analytical symphony, your digital marketing efforts will gain a deep understanding of the impact and ROI of influencer collaborations. Like a conductor orchestrating a harmonious performance, your data-driven approach will refine influencer marketing strategies, enabling you to strike the right chords and resonate with your audience effectively.

* * *

CHAPTER 9: DATA ANALYTICS AND PERFORMANCE MEASUREMENT

Implementing Analytics Tools For Tracking And Analyzing Data

Implementing analytic tools for tracking and analyzing data in your digital marketing is akin to equipping your marketing arsenal with high-powered telescopes and fine-tuned instruments, enabling you to explore the vast universe of insights and performance metrics. Picture yourself as an astute astronomer, using cutting-edge tools to uncover valuable data that illuminates the path to marketing success.

1. Define Your Stargazing Objectives: Begin by defining your stargazing objectives, much like an astronomer selecting celestial targets. Determine the specific metrics and goals you want to track, such as website traffic, conversions, click-through rates, or social media engagement.

2. Choose the Right Analytic Constellations: Select the right analytic tools, like constellations guiding your journey through data galaxies. Platforms such as Google Analytics, social media insights, and email marketing metrics offer comprehensive data to analyze.

3. Integrate Tools for a Unified Sky Map: Integrate your analytic tools, much like a unified sky map that brings all data into one view. Connect your website, social media accounts, and email marketing platforms to access a cohesive overview of your digital universe.

4. Explore Customer Journey Trajectories: Explore the trajectories of your customer journey, akin to mapping celestial paths. Use analytics to trace user behavior from entry to conversion, gaining insights into touchpoints and identifying potential areas for improvement.

5. Observe Stellar Performance Metrics: Observe stellar performance metrics, like distant stars providing valuable information. Track key indicators such as bounce rates, time on page, conversion rates, and ROI to assess the effectiveness of your campaigns.

6. Discover Constellations of Audience Insights: Discover constellations of audience insights, akin to studying star clusters for patterns. Analyze demographic data, interests, and behavior to understand your audience better and tailor your marketing strategies accordingly.

7. Monitor Orbiting Social Media Engagement: Monitor orbiting social media engagement, much like observing planets in motion. Track likes, shares, comments, and sentiment to measure brand impact and refine your social media content approach.

8. Measure the Gravity of Email Campaigns: Measure the gravity of email campaigns, like quantifying the gravitational pull of your content. Analyze open rates, click-through rates, and conversion rates to optimize email marketing performance.

9. Perform Astronomical A/B Testing: Conduct astronomical A/B testing, like conducting experiments in the cosmos of marketing. Test different variables, such as ad copy, visuals, or landing page designs, to identify winning combinations that boost results.

10. Navigate the Data Universe and Adapt: Navigate the data universe like an agile astronomer, adjusting your trajectory as needed. Continuously monitor, analyze, and interpret data to adapt your digital marketing strategies and propel your campaigns to new heights.

By implementing analytic tools like a skilled astronomer exploring the cosmic expanse, your digital marketing efforts will gain valuable insights and guidance. Like mapping the stars, your data-driven approach will navigate you towards marketing success, enabling you to make informed decisions and steer your brand towards growth and stellar performance.

Interpreting Key Performance Indicators (KPIs) And Metrics

Interpreting key performance indicators (KPIs) and metrics is akin to unraveling the intricate threads of a tapestry, where each pattern and color holds a story that reveals the performance narrative of your digital marketing efforts. Picture yourself as a skilled weaver, meticulously examining each thread to understand the full picture and make informed decisions.

1. Define the Context of Your Tapestry: Begin by defining the context of your tapestry, like setting the stage for interpretation. Understand the objectives of your digital marketing campaigns and align them with the relevant KPIs and metrics to ensure a clear focus.

2. Identify the Vibrant Patterns of Success: Identify the vibrant patterns of success woven into your data, like spotting standout elements that shine. Look for positive trends, spikes, or consistent growth in KPIs that indicate areas of achievement and strength.

3. Untangle the Threads of Underperformance: Untangle the threads of underperformance, much like addressing areas that need improvement. Identify declining trends or low-performing metrics and pinpoint potential reasons to formulate actionable strategies for enhancement.

4. Weave Insights Across Multiple Metrics: Weave insights across multiple metrics, like blending various colors to create a harmonious design. Analyze how different KPIs relate to one another, understanding their impact on overall performance and their interconnectedness.

5. Recognize the Story Each Metric Tells: Recognize the unique story each metric tells, akin to understanding individual threads' significance. For example, click-through rates reveal audience engagement, conversion rates signify customer actions, and bounce rates reflect content relevance.

6. Consider Seasonal and Trending Elements: Factor in seasonal and trending elements, like incorporating shifting patterns into your interpretation. Recognize how external factors may influence KPIs, ensuring a comprehensive understanding of performance fluctuations.

7. Compare Against Benchmarks as Your Standard Measures: Compare your metrics against benchmarks as your standard measures, akin to gauging your tapestry's quality. Utilize industry standards, historical data, or competitor insights to assess your performance against established norms.

8. Combine Qualitative and Quantitative Insights: Blend qualitative and quantitative insights, like weaving together texture and color. Supplement your data analysis with customer feedback, surveys, and focus groups to gain a deeper understanding of the audience's perception.

9. Visualize Data as a Masterpiece: Visualize your data as a masterpiece, like admiring a completed tapestry. Use data visualization tools to present your insights clearly and artistically, making it easier to communicate findings to stakeholders and drive data-informed decisions.

10. Evolve and Adapt with the Changing Weave: Embrace continuous learning and adaptation, like evolving your tapestry with time. Stay updated with industry trends, experiment with new metrics, and be open to evolving your KPIs as your digital marketing strategy grows.

By interpreting KPIs and metrics with the artistry of a skilled weaver, your digital marketing efforts will be guided by data-driven insights. Like a tapestry that reflects careful craftsmanship, your interpretation will help you create a cohesive and successful strategy, ensuring your marketing masterpiece continues to evolve and captivate your audience.

Optimizing Campaigns Based On Data-Driven Insights

Optimizing campaigns for your digital marketing based on data-driven insights is akin to crafting a finely tuned symphony, where every note is meticulously orchestrated to create harmonious and impactful performances. Picture yourself as a discerning conductor, using data as your musical score to guide the refinement of your marketing strategies.

1. Start with a Data Sonata: Begin your optimization journey with a data sonata, exploring insights from various sources like a melody unfolding. Analyze key performance indicators, audience behavior, and customer feedback to identify patterns and opportunities.

2. Listen to Your Audience as the Primary Melody: Listen to your audience as the primary melody, like the captivating voice that directs your

composition. Pay attention to their preferences, pain points, and needs, using data to tailor your campaigns to resonate with them.

3. Harmonize Data Sources for Comprehensive Insights: Harmonize data sources for comprehensive insights, like different instruments playing in unison. Combine data from website analytics, social media metrics, email performance, and sales data to gain a holistic view.

4. Conduct A/B Tests as Your Crescendos: Conduct A/B tests as your crescendos, experimenting with variations to discover what resonates most. Test different ad creatives, landing pages, or audience segments, allowing data to reveal the most effective approaches.

5. Identify High-Performing Channels as Your Key Players: Identify high-performing channels as your key players, like virtuoso musicians showcasing their talents. Focus on channels that drive the most significant results and allocate resources accordingly for maximum impact.

6. Fine-Tune Content Composition for Each Segment: Fine-tune content composition for each segment, like crafting personalized melodies for different audiences. Utilize data to tailor messages, visuals, and offers to address the unique needs and interests of specific customer segments.

7. Optimize Budget Allocation Like a Skilled Conductor: Optimize budget allocation like a skilled conductor balancing instruments' prominence in a symphony. Allocate budget based on data insights, directing more resources to high-converting channels and campaigns.

8. Iterative Improvisation for Ongoing Refinement: Embrace iterative improvisation, continuously refining your marketing strategies based on data feedback. Monitor performance regularly, learn from successes and challenges, and adapt your tactics accordingly.

9. Analyze Conversion Funnels as Your Cadences: Analyze conversion funnels as your cadences, understanding where your audience progresses smoothly or encounters stumbling blocks. Use data to streamline the customer journey, optimizing conversion paths and minimizing drop-offs.

10. Measure ROI as Your Standing Ovation: Measure ROI as your standing ovation, celebrating the success of your optimized campaigns. Analyze the impact of data-driven adjustments, recognizing how they contribute to the overall success of your digital marketing symphony.

By optimizing campaigns with data-driven insights like a skillful conductor, your digital marketing efforts will achieve a harmonious balance of efficiency and effectiveness. Like a symphony that evolves and refines with each performance, your data-driven approach will ensure continuous improvement and elevate your marketing efforts to crescendos of success.

* * *

CHAPTER 10: FUTURE TRENDS AND INNOVATIONS IN DIGITAL MARKETING

Exploring Emerging Technologies And Their Impact On Marketing

Exploring emerging technologies and their impact on digital marketing is akin to embarking on an exhilarating quest to uncharted territories, where you embrace innovation as your compass and curiosity as your guide. Picture yourself as a trailblazing explorer, venturing into the realm of cutting-edge technologies that shape the future of marketing.

1. Embrace Curiosity as Your Expedition's Starting Point: Begin your exploration with curiosity as your expedition's starting point, akin to setting sail with an insatiable thirst for knowledge. Be open to new ideas, emerging trends, and unconventional approaches that challenge the status quo.

2. Navigate the Technological Landscape with Purpose: Navigate the vast technological landscape with purpose, just as a skilled cartographer charts unexplored territories. Identify emerging technologies, such as AI, VR, blockchain, or voice assistants, and their potential implications for digital marketing.

3. Experiment with Innovative Prototypes as Your Exploratory Tools: Experiment with innovative prototypes as your exploratory tools, testing the

waters of new technologies. Conduct pilot projects, proof-of-concepts, or small-scale campaigns to gauge their feasibility and impact.

4. Observe Industry Pioneers as Your Guiding Stars: Observe industry pioneers as your guiding stars, seeking inspiration from early adopters and trailblazers. Study case studies and success stories to learn how others leverage emerging technologies in their digital marketing endeavors.

5. Adopt Agile Learning as Your Adventurous Spirit: Embrace agile learning as your adventurous spirit, welcoming constant adaptation and evolution. Stay informed through industry publications, webinars, workshops, and networking to keep abreast of emerging trends.

6. Identify Technology-Driven Audience Behavior as Your Footprints: Identify technology-driven changes in audience behavior as your footprints, signaling shifts in preferences and interactions. Use data analytics to understand how emerging technologies impact customer journeys.

7. Leverage Data-Driven Insights as Your Valuable Compass: Leverage data-driven insights as your valuable compass, guiding your decisions with concrete evidence. Analyze performance metrics, user feedback, and market research to inform your approach.

8. Collaborate with Innovative Partners as Your Fellow Explorers: Collaborate with innovative partners as your fellow explorers, expanding your horizons through mutually beneficial ventures. Partner with tech startups, creative agencies, or industry disruptors to explore new frontiers together.

9. Cultivate an Adaptive Culture as Your Exploration Expedition: Cultivate an adaptive culture within your organization, fostering a spirit of continuous learning and innovation. Encourage creativity, experimentation, and a growth mindset to embrace emerging technologies fearlessly.

10. Visualize a Tech-Infused Future as Your Destination: Envision a tech-infused future as your destination, mapping out the potential impact of

emerging technologies on digital marketing. Use your insights to create a forward-thinking strategy that prepares your brand for the journey ahead.

By exploring emerging technologies with the spirit of an intrepid adventurer, your digital marketing efforts will stay ahead of the curve and embrace opportunities for innovation. Like an exploration expedition that uncovers new horizons, your willingness to embrace emerging technologies will fuel your marketing success and propel your brand into a tech-driven future.

Understanding The Importance Of AI, Voice Search, And Chatbots

Understanding the importance of AI, voice search, and chatbots for your digital marketing is akin to unlocking a trinity of transformative tools that empower your brand to connect with your audience in remarkable ways. Picture yourself as a visionary architect, designing a cutting-edge digital landscape where AI, voice search, and chatbots form the pillars of an immersive and personalized customer experience.

1. AI: The Intelligent Foundation: Imagine AI as the intelligent foundation of your digital marketing strategy, where data-driven insights and automation converge. AI algorithms analyze vast amounts of data, enabling you to understand your audience on a granular level, predict trends, and deliver hyper-personalized content.

2. Voice Search: The Resonant Gateway: Consider voice search as the resonant gateway to your audience's needs, preferences, and queries. With the rising popularity of voice assistants like Siri, Alexa, and Google Assistant, optimizing your content for voice search ensures you're present in the hands-free interactions of your customers.

3. Chatbots: The Interactive Allies: Visualize chatbots as interactive allies that cater to your audience's real-time inquiries and support needs. These conversational agents offer immediate responses, enhancing customer service, and streamlining user experiences, leading to higher satisfaction and engagement.

4. AI-Driven Personalization: The Tailored Experience: Embrace AI-driven personalization as the essence of delivering tailored experiences to your audience. By understanding individual preferences, behaviors, and purchase history, you can curate content, offers, and recommendations that resonate with each customer.

5. Voice Search SEO: The Audible Optimization: Consider voice search SEO as the audible optimization that positions your brand in voice assistant results. Crafting content with natural language and featured snippets in mind boosts your visibility in voice search queries, driving organic traffic and brand recognition.

6. Chatbot Integration: The Always-On Support: Integrate chatbots as the always-on support that provides 24/7 assistance to your audience. Whether answering FAQs, helping with order inquiries, or providing product recommendations, chatbots enrich the customer journey and nurture loyalty.

7. AI-Enhanced Data Analysis: The Predictive Advantage: Leverage AI-enhanced data analysis as your predictive advantage in the dynamic market landscape. By harnessing AI algorithms to interpret customer behavior and market trends, you can make data-driven decisions that lead to competitive advantages.

8. Voice-Enabled Customer Engagement: The Conversational Touchpoints: Embrace voice-enabled customer engagement as the conversational touchpoints that forge meaningful connections. Creating voice-activated content, such as podcasts or voice-guided tutorials, enables immersive interactions with your brand.

9. Chatbot-Enabled Lead Nurturing: The Relationship Builder: Utilize chatbot-enabled lead nurturing as the relationship builder that guides prospects through the sales funnel. Tailoring chatbot interactions based on customer behavior nurtures leads, converting them into loyal advocates.

10. AI-Powered Insights: The Compass for Growth: Consider AI-powered insights as the compass that navigates your digital marketing growth. From dynamic content optimization to predictive customer segmentation, AI empowers you to continuously innovate and stay ahead of the competition.

By understanding the pivotal roles of AI, voice search, and chatbots in your digital marketing, your brand can embrace the transformative potential of these tools. Like a visionary architect sculpting a digital masterpiece, your strategic integration of AI, voice search, and chatbots will craft an immersive and customer-centric landscape that resonates with your audience and propels your brand to new heights.

Adapting Strategies For A Constantly Evolving Digital Landscape

Adapting strategies for a constantly evolving digital landscape in your digital marketing is akin to becoming an agile navigator, charting a course that embraces change and thrives in uncharted waters. Picture yourself as a resilient captain, steering your marketing ship with innovation and versatility as your compass.

1. Embrace Dynamic Flexibility as Your Sailing Philosophy: Embrace dynamic flexibility as your sailing philosophy, adjusting your strategies with the changing tides. Remain open to adopting emerging technologies, exploring new platforms, and fine-tuning your approach as needed.

2. Cultivate a Growth Mindset as Your Wind of Change: Cultivate a growth mindset as your wind of change, propelling you forward despite

uncertainties. Encourage a culture of continuous learning, experimentation, and risk-taking, empowering your team to embrace opportunities and challenges.

3. Leverage Real-Time Data Insights as Your Navigational Tool: Leverage real-time data insights as your navigational tool, guiding your decision-making in the digital ocean. Monitor performance metrics, customer behavior, and market trends to make data-driven adjustments swiftly.

4. Strive for Personalized Engagement as Your Destination: Strive for personalized engagement as your destination, recognizing the value of tailored experiences. Utilize AI-driven data analysis to understand individual preferences, enabling you to deliver content that resonates with your audience.

5. Create Omni-Channel Presence as Your Expansive Horizon: Create omni-channel presence as your expansive horizon, reaching your audience wherever they roam. Seamlessly integrate your marketing efforts across platforms, ensuring a consistent brand experience and expanding your reach.

6. Optimize for Voice Search as Your Sonic Navigation: Optimize for voice search as your sonic navigation, acknowledging the rising influence of voice assistants. Craft content with natural language, featured snippets, and conversational keywords to be readily discoverable in voice searches.

7. Implement Conversational AI as Your Crew Support: Implement conversational AI as your crew support, enhancing customer interactions with chatbots. These virtual assistants provide 24/7 support, streamlining user experiences and nurturing leads through automated engagement.

8. Collaborate with Innovative Partners as Your Expedition Allies: Collaborate with innovative partners as your expedition allies, uniting forces to navigate the ever-changing digital landscape. Partner with tech startups, influencers, or industry disruptors to uncover new opportunities and inspire creative initiatives.

9. Monitor Competitors as Your Celestial Navigation: Monitor competitors as your celestial navigation, understanding market dynamics and staying ahead of the competition. Analyze their strategies, successes, and failures to inform your own course of action.

10. Stay Ahead with Trendspotting as Your Radar: Stay ahead with trendspotting as your radar, detecting emerging trends and opportunities before they become mainstream. Keep a keen eye on industry developments, consumer behavior shifts, and technological advancements to remain a pioneer in your field.

By adopting these agile strategies, you'll navigate the constantly evolving digital landscape with confidence and ingenuity. Like a seasoned captain leading your marketing ship, you'll thrive amidst change, seize new horizons, and propel your brand towards sustained success in the dynamic waters of digital marketing.

Conclusion:

"Digital Marketing Accelerated: A Marketer's Guide To Success" equips you with the knowledge, skills, and strategies to navigate the dynamic world of digital marketing successfully. By embracing the tools and techniques outlined in this book, you'll gain a competitive edge and position your business for sustained growth and success in the digital era. Get ready to unlock the full potential of digital marketing and become a true master of the craft.

Best Of Luck In All Of Your Marketing Endeavors!

Dack Douglas

And as an added bonus, scan the QR code below and get 10% off every t-shirt purchase. Simply apply the code BOOK at checkout.